HERO JOURNALS

Geronimo

Richard Spilsbury

Chicago, Illinois

Edited by Adam Miller, Charlotte Guillain, and
Claire Throp
Designed by Richard Parker and Ken Vail Graphic
Design
Original illustrations © Capstone Global Library
Ltd 2014
Illustrated by Florence Faure
Picture research Tracy Cummins
Production by Victoria Fitzgerald
Originated by Capstone Global Library Ltd
Printed and bound in China by Leo Paper
Products Ltd

17 16 15 14 13
10 9 8 7 6 5 4 3 2 1

**Library of Congress Cataloging-in-Publication
Data**
Spilsbury, Richard, 1963-
  Geronimo / Richard Spilsbury.
    p. cm.—(Hero journals)
  Includes bibliographical references and index.
  ISBN 978-1-4109-5360-5 (hb)—ISBN 978-1-4109-
5367-4 (pb)
1. Geronimo, 1829-1909—Juvenile literature. 2.
Apache Indians—Kings and rulers—Biography—
Juvenile literature. 3. Apache Indians—Wars—
Juvenile literature. I. Title.
  E99.A6G32742 2014
  979.004'97250092—dc23   2012043525

Acknowledgments
We would like to thank the following for
permission to reproduce photographs: Alamy
pp. 6 (© World History Archive), 15 (© Robert
Harding World Imagery); Bridgeman Art Library
pp. 21 (© Look and Learn), 25 (Frederic (1861-
1909) / Private Collection); Corbis pp. 24 (©
Bettmann), 33, 34 (© Corbis); Getty Images pp.
5, 17 (Archive Photos), 22-23 (Time Life Pictures/
National Archives), 28 (Transcendental Graphics),
31, 36 (MPI), 39 (Lawrence Migdale); Library of
Congress Prints and Photographs pp. 4, 9, 11, 13,
37, 38; Nativestock Pictures pp. 19, 27 (© Marilyn
Angel Wynn); Shutterstock p. 30 (© Caitlin Mirra)

Design elements supplied by Shutterstock (©
R-studio), (© Pavel K), (© Picsfive), (© karawan).

Cover photograph of Geronimo reproduced with
permission of Gettty Images (Archive Photos).

We would like to thank Strother Roberts for his
invaluable help in the preparation of this book.

Every effort has been made to contact copyright
holders of material reproduced in this book. Any
omissions will be rectified in subsequent printings
if notice is given to the publisher.

All the Internet addresses (URLs) given in this
book were valid at the time of going to press.
However, due to the dynamic nature of the
Internet, some addresses may have changed,
or sites may have changed or ceased to exist
since publication. While the author and publisher
regret any inconvenience this may cause readers,
no responsibility for any such changes can be
accepted by either the author or the publisher.

Contents

I Am Geronimo

My chest is tight and it is difficult to breathe. I am an old man, lying here in this bed, feeling very tired. Reading the record of my life, I am transported back to how I felt as a boy, growing into a man. My heart is racing as I think of my adventures, the blood I spilled, the look of fear in men's eyes, and the war cries of the Apache people. I wonder, could I have done things differently?

> *"I was born on the prairies where the wind blew free and there was nothing to break the light of the Sun. I was born where there were no enclosures."*
>
> Geronimo

I might be nearing the end of my life, but I am still the man who once led brave Apaches into battle.

Chiricahua leader

I am Geronimo, warrior and leader of the Chiricahuas. My childhood name was Goyathlay, and when I was young, we rode and hunted on Chiricahua lands, as our forefathers had before us. But life has changed through the years, like my name. I have fought many battles with my Apache brothers and struggled to get what we needed to survive and to stay free. Make no mistake, people far and wide fear and respect the Apaches.

The Apache tribes are all different, but we mostly stood together as brothers in our battles to survive.

Apache people

In Geronimo's time, the Apaches were divided into seven tribes. One tribe was called Chiricahua. Geronimo was the leader of one band within the Chiricahuas called the Bedonkohes. Other Chiricahua bands included Chokonen, Nedni, and Chihene.

My Early Years

I was born in June 1829. My home is in No-Doyohn Canyon, among the high mountains. This is near the head of the mighty Gila River in Mexico. My father is Taklishim, son of the great Bedonkohe chief Mahko. My mother is Juana. My parents gave me the name Goyathlay.

> "I was warmed by the Sun, rocked by the winds, and sheltered by the trees as other Indian babes."
>
> Geronimo

Document it!

This journal follows Geronimo's story from his birth onward, but you can organize your journal in a different way. For example, you could divide it up into themes such as friends, family, and trips.

My mother says I slept peacefully as a baby. In Apache language, *Goyathlay* means "One Who Yawns"!

Blood brothers

The lands of my Bedonkohe people lie next to the lands of our blood brothers. These bands are our good friends and fight alongside the Bedonkohe. The Chokonen, led by Cochise, and the Nedni live to the south. Our great chief is Mangas Coloradas. He holds many councils with their leaders, and we visit each others' camps often. We are not so friendly with the White Mountain Apaches from the north.

Geronimo's siblings

Geronimo wrote that he had three brothers and four sisters, but historians think that only one of these was an actual sister. They believe the rest were cousins. There was no word in the Apache language to distinguish "cousin" from "brother" or "sister." Geronimo sometimes called his nephews "brothers," too.

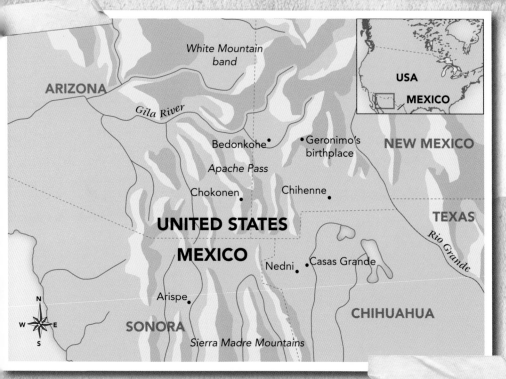

We lived in the dry mountains and valleys around the U.S.-Mexico border.

Home life

I spend most of my days with my brothers and sisters and other Chiricahua children. My best friend, Juh of the Nedni band, is one of them. We care for the horses and practice riding them near the camp. But we love to get out into the wilderness. Here we track rabbits, play hide and seek, and shoot targets with our bows and arrows.

We live in a group of tepees with my aunts and their daughters and families. These are different than the dome-shaped wickiups made from grass and sticks that other Chiricahua live in.

A tepee starts with a tripod of strong sticks tied at the top. We rest other sticks on that and then cover it with a semicircular sheet of sewn skins.

Food and farming

Sometimes my mother makes me help collect food from our family plot in the communal field. Here we grow beans, pumpkins, maize (corn) to make bread, and tobacco for the adults to smoke. We help to gather nuts and berries, herbs to make medicines, and mescal from the wild. The men hunt deer and sometimes buffalo for us to eat, too.

Buffalo

There were once tens of millions of buffalo on the grassy plains. The Apaches hunted only those they needed for meat and for skins to make tepees and clothes. In the 19th century, white settlers started killing huge numbers of buffalo, and by the end of the century they were nearly extinct.

We collect water from streams and rivers, and the containers are carried by our horses.

Joining in ceremonies

I know about our great people from my parents. My father tells me tales of amazing Apache victories and great hunts in the past. One day, I hope I can be a leader like my grandfather, Chief Mahko. My mother tells me how the Apache people came to this Earth. She teaches me how to pray to *Usen*. *Usen* is the god or "life giver" for our people. *Usen* helps the chief make good decisions and helps us care for others.

Creation of the Apache

The Apache believe that in the beginning the world was dark, and eagles led birds in battle with bows and arrows against beasts to bring light to the world. The beasts destroyed all human babies except one. He was hidden by his mother and grew up to defeat the last beast. He was the first Apache.

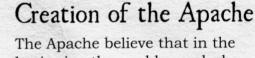

My people wear eagle feathers to celebrate the wisdom and power of the bird that helped our tribe come into being.

My first ceremony

Today, we celebrated our god Usen. The adults wore amazing costumes and there was dancing. We have many different ceremonies. Some are to awaken the animal spirits who watch over us and others are to make rain fall on our crops so harvests are bountiful. I remember my first ceremony when I could barely walk; my mother gave me new moccasins to walk a trail of flower pollen leading east. She says this symbolizes a long and successful life.

Document it!

Geronimo and other Apache took part in many ceremonies in their lives. In your journal, write down what happens at the ceremonies you attend, such as weddings. Who was involved? What was the order of events?

I was mesmerized when watching the dancers' movements and listening to their chanting during ceremonies, just as my forefathers must have been.

Death of Jaklishim

My father, Jaklishim, died. He had suffered from a long sickness, and my mother cared for him as best she could. After his last breath passed, elders in our clan closed my father's eyes with clay and put him in his best clothes. They wrapped a colorful blanket around him and tied him on his horse. My mother and aunts wailed as our family walked behind the horse to a secret cave. Here we buried him under stones, with his weapons by his side.

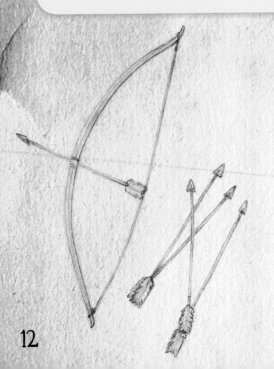

> *"Wrapped in splendor he lies in seclusion, and the winds in the pines sing a low requiem over the dead warrior."*
>
> Geronimo on his father's death

Document it!

Even sad events in your life such as family deaths are important records of your history, how ceremonies were conducted, and how you felt at the time. Your notes will be fascinating to your family and maybe others in the future.

Caring for my mother

We have just moved into a new tepee because we burned my father's after his death. It is the Chiricahua way. My mother says she will not marry again, even though our people allow it after two or three years. Anyway, I am old enough to look after my mother, brothers, and sisters. I am 15 now and strong from farming our plot.

My life as head of the home gives me lots of responsibility and is hard work. But we sometimes take trips away to stay in the rougher country farther south, among the Nedni. It is always a pleasure to stay with Juh and his wife, Ishton, my cousin.

Our tepees look like these. They are easy to pack up when we move.

Becoming a Man

I have been following the chase to learn how men hunt since I was about 10. I watched them ride quickly on horseback and use spears to bring down large buffalo. It takes skill not to be knocked off and trampled or gored. Now I hunt alone and with my friends.

Horses and Apaches

In 1680, a rebellion by Pueblo Indians in New Mexico sent Spanish settlers fleeing. Many horses left behind lived wild in huge herds. The Apaches tamed and bred horses and traded them with other tribes. By the 18th century, the Apaches were expert riders who fought and hunted from horseback.

Ways of hunting

Deer are tricky to catch. We cover ourselves in deer fat and wear deerskins so that we smell and look like deer from a distance. We crawl slowly toward them, but the deer often spot us anyway. It's more fun to hunt turkeys. We ride after them to where they hide in forests. Then we bash them with sticks when they suddenly fly up!

Sometimes we hunt to prove our bravery. Today, I killed a bear in its den. I was not scared, but I know its claws could have ripped me apart. When people see the skin I brought back, they realize I am a great hunter.

I have even climbed in the high mountains to hunt a great eagle for its white feathers.

"It required great skill to steal upon an eagle, for besides having sharp eyes, he is wise and never stops at any place where he does not have a good view of the surrounding country."

Geronimo

Training and testing

Early this morning, I had to swim in the river again. The shock of the ice-cold water took my breath away. This is one of the challenges the adults set us teenagers to make us fit and strong and to prepare us for life as men. Sometimes we have to run to a distant hilltop with a mouthful of water, so we can only breathe through our noses. We also have contests in shooting and wrestling.

Hoop and pole

Hoop and pole was a traditional Apache game. Men tried to knock over a rolling wooden hoop by throwing a spear through it. Contestants scored more points if the hoop fell closer to the rear end of the spear. Warriors gambled on who would win.

Council of Warriors

It is 1846, and I am now 17 years old. Today, the Council of Warriors summoned me. I am so excited—the council is at last satisfied that I have proved my strength, courage, and ingenuity in all those tests. I am now a warrior, too. Being a warrior gives me the freedom to go where I choose and do what I want. Now I can join the other warriors in real fights.

Document it!

Fitness was important for Geronimo's survival as a warrior, but it is important for your health, too. In your journal, keep a record of what sports you play and what exercise you get. It will be interesting to read about in the future.

All that preparation and fitness training were worthwhile. I am now ready to fight in men's battles.

Jaking a wife

Now that I am a warrior, I can marry. I have been very close to a Nedni maiden named Alope for many years. We have spent a lot of time together alone. But before I could marry her, I had to get permission from her father, Noposo. He is a stubborn man and demanded a payment of many ponies in return for her hand in marriage. I did not like to do it, but I had to take the animals from the family herd that my father took many years to build up. Still, it is done. Noposo has handed over his daughter to me. There was no ceremony, but now we are husband and wife at last.

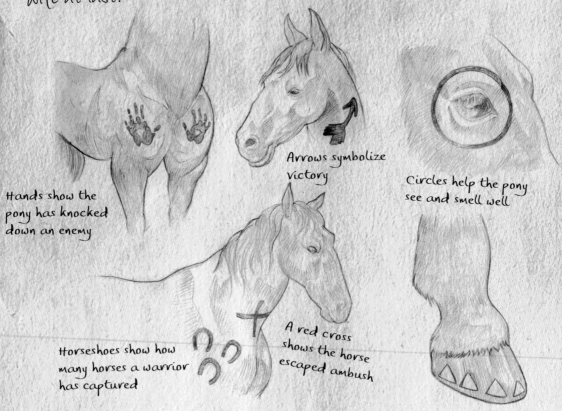

Hands show the pony has knocked down an enemy

Arrows symbolize victory

Circles help the pony see and smell well

Horseshoes show how many horses a warrior has captured

A red cross shows the horse escaped ambush

Yellow triangles make the horse run fast without stumbling

We believe that paint marks can help horses and also symbolize the achievements of rider and horse.

Setting up home

I am a very happy man. I built a new tepee near my mother's for Alope and me in the Bedonkohe settlement. Alope decorated it inside with bear robes, lion hides, and other trophies of my hunts. She drew pictures on buckskin and made sacred hoops decorated with beads for the walls. I love her dearly, and since we have been husband and wife, we have had three children together.

Medicine wheel

The medicine wheel or sacred hoop is a symbol that many American Indians, including the Apaches, believed had the power to heal and protect. It represents the circle of life. Its four colors—black, white, yellow, and green or red—show the four seasons and four directions (forward, back, left, and right).

Mexican Enemies

We often travel just over the Mexican border to trade with villagers there for things we need, such as food. It is mostly peaceful between our peoples. But sometimes Apaches attack villages to take what they want. There is fighting, and people from both sides can die. Now there are more Mexican troops roaming the countryside who are suspicious of any Apaches, even when we go there simply to trade. They attack us without warning. I have even heard that their government ordered troops to kill and scalp any Apaches they find.

buffalo jawbone war club

Scalping

Scalping is when people cut skin with hair attached from someone's head as proof the person is dead. Scalping is commonly associated with American Indians, but it was done just as much by Mexicans. In some Mexican and U.S. states, the government offered money for each Apache scalp handed in.

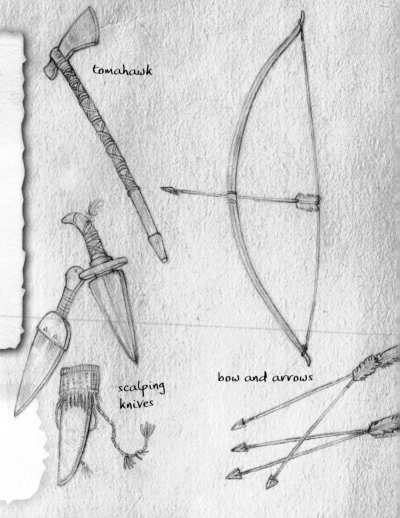

tomahawk

scalping knives

bow and arrows

These are some of the weapons we use for fighting.

Massacre at Janos

A large party of Bedonkohe and Nedni went to Casas Grande in Mexico to trade. I brought my family. We set up our tepees outside town. During the day, groups of us men went into town to trade. When we returned, we discovered that Mexican troops had attacked the camp. Among the dead women and children lie my dear Alope, my children, and my mother. I am numb with shock, but on this day in 1858, I vow to avenge their deaths.

"Whenever I came near…or saw anything to remind me of former happy days, my heart would ache for revenge upon Mexico."

Geronimo

The Mexicans are now our enemies.

On the war path

Our chief, Mangas-Coloradas, called a council of war to fight the Mexicans. At his request, I persuaded Cochise of the Chokonen and Juh of the Nedni to help us. Now our bands are grouped together at the Mexican border. Our faces are painted and we wear the bands of war around our heads. We are prepared to die in battle. But in case we do not return, our families will be in hiding when the Mexican troops come searching for them.

Cochise

Cochise was leader of the Chokonen Chiricahua. In his early adult life, Cochise was a woodcutter, but he became a warrior after six innocent Apaches were hanged by U.S. troops in 1861. He often fought alongside Geronimo and was military leader of the Apaches up to his death in 1874.

In this photograph, you can just see Geronimo standing in front of Chief Naiche (Chokonen) on horseback.

Ambush and glory

We hid in the woods near the town of Arispe and captured Mexican scouts with supplies, including more guns. The next morning, we ambushed and surrounded the army. I led the battle, and we slaughtered them all. A giant war whoop of victory echoed outside Arispe before we scalped their soldiers.

> "Still covered with the blood of my enemies, still holding my conquering weapon, still hot with the joy of battle, victory, and vengeance, I was surrounded by the Apache braves and made war chief of all the Apache...I could not call back my loved ones, I could not bring back the dead Apache, but I could rejoice in this revenge."
>
> Geronimo

Becoming Geronimo

The battle at Arispe has changed my life. I am now a trusted Apache leader. My name has changed, too. When the Mexican soldiers were losing, they pleaded for help from their Saint Jerome—Jeronimo. When other Mexicans saw me on the battlefield leading the Apaches and heard Jeronimo, they thought it was my name. Now other Apaches call me Geronimo, too!

Geronimo's wives

After Alope's death, Geronimo married Cheehashkish and then took a second wife, Nanathathtith. Apache leaders sometimes had more than one wife. Geronimo had eight wives, but never more than two at once. Nanathathtith was killed. Three wives, including Cheehashkish, were captured during battles with Mexicans. Geronimo had eight children.

The Apaches and the Mexicans now know what Geronimo is capable of. I shall never be Goyathlay again.

Raids into Mexico

Raiding is now our way of life. We steal what we can from Mexican villages, from sugar to cattle. In one village, Crassanas, the Apache cries alone drove the people away, and we helped ourselves from the village stores. But today, I was lucky to survive the fighting. I was hit with a Mexican's gun after slipping on a pool of blood in a fight. Luckily, another Apache speared him before he could deliver the final blow. We just managed to escape. I now have a scar on my head to remind me.

Here, we are returning from a raid into Mexico.

Document it!

Many American Indians felt that stealing was often their only option to get what they needed. Remember that events relate to the times they happened, so in your journal, give some context or idea of what life is like in your times.

White Settlers

Since the 1850s, more and more white settlers have come to Arizona. We traded with them peacefully at first, but after gold miners started to attack us, we raided their settlements, too. The U.S. troops were already wary of us. These tensions eased during the Civil War, beginning in 1861, because all the troops disappeared east to fight their own people. But now they are returning in greater numbers, and life is getting tougher for the Apaches.

The move into Mexico from the mid-19th century brought in more white settlers to the area where Chiricahuas lived and put more pressure on shared space and resources.

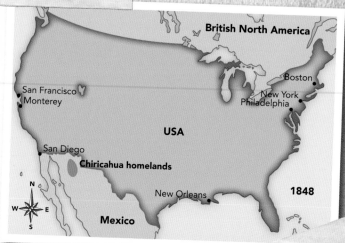

An expanding country

During the 19th century, the United States grew by gaining territory from Mexico. White American settlers moved in to find land for farming and to search for gold. The newcomers forced American Indian tribes from their lands, causing great conflict. The U.S. government tried to ease tensions by setting up areas of land just for the tribes, called reservations, but typically these lands were not as good for farming and hunting.

Tricked

The U.S. government offered blankets, flour, beef, and all kinds of supplies if the Bedonkohe moved to land in New Mexico and stopped fighting. I said it was too good to be true, but Mangas-Coloradas went to make peace. Our great leader was captured and killed. We have called a council of war, and I, Geronimo, have become chief of the Bedonkohe.

Mangas-Coloradas

Mangas-Coloradas was Bedonkohe leader from 1837. He signed a peace treaty with the U.S. government in 1848, after the government had taken New Mexico. But violence against Apaches by settlers led him to break the treaty and join other leaders in years of struggle against the white Americans, before his death in 1863.

Moving around

It is getting trickier to avoid capture because the U.S. Army has trained a group of Apaches to help track us! This winter is very cold and food is hard to find, so we have come to live at the new Chiricahua reservation at Apache Pass, near Bedonhoke lands in Arizona. We made a peace treaty with General Howard. He gives us good rations, clothing, and other supplies in return for staying. But there are troubles brewing among the Apaches, and I am not sure how long the Bedonkohes can stay here.

U. S. Apache Scouts.

These are desperate times. Why else would our Apache brothers use their tribal skills to help the U.S. Army hunt me and my people?

Apache scouts

The U.S. Army had difficulty tracking Apaches who refused to recognize the authority of the U.S. government (such as Geronimo) in the wild, mountainous terrain of Arizona. So they recruited White Mountain Apaches as scouts to help them. This band of Apaches had the same excellent tracking skills as other Apaches, but they did not mind using them against their people, since they were not friendly with other Chiricahua bands.

Arrested

In 1876, the U.S. government ordered all Chiricahua tribespeople except army scouts to move to San Carlos Reservation, in eastern Arizona. They arrested me and other Bedonkohes for leaving Apache Pass and moved us to San Carlos. But we could not live there—it is a dry, barren desert. Now I am on the run with my family and a band of Bedonkohes and Nedni in the Sierra Madre Mountains. But the scouts are never far behind us.

Life on the run was not easy for us.

Trouble in Mexico

First, we were chased by U.S. troops who wanted to arrest us for escaping San Carlos, and then by Mexican troops because we went into Mexico to raid. In 1880, we were attacked by Mexican troops, and 12 Apaches were killed. We tried to make peace with them—we even shook hands and drank together—but we were still attacked. We had to run like dogs into the hills.

Life in the high mountains was hard, but from there we could see our enemy approaching better and find secret hiding places.

The last Mexican battle

It could have been the end for us because we were careless. When the Mexican troops attacked us, we were camped in the open in a deep channel with ditches leading from it. There was no choice but to hide in the ditches, since we were outnumbered. Then, their general started talking to his troops, and I crawled near him in my ditch. I stood and shot him. In return, many Mexicans fired at me, but amazingly none hit me. The Apaches took this as a sign of victory and attacked. This forced the Mexican troops back, and we set fire to the grasses between them and us. In the smoke, we escaped.

"The soldiers never explained to the government when an Indian was wronged, but reported the misdeeds of the Indians. We took an oath not to do any wrong to each other or to scheme against each other."

Geronimo

There aren't very many of us left now, and it is more difficult to dodge the Mexican bullets when they have so many more men than we do.

Years on the run

In the early 1880s, we were a group of around 250 Chiricahua on the run in Mexico. Since then, the battles and fights have shrunk our numbers. Many, including my comrade, Juh, are dead; other Chiricahua have been captured. Now there are just 40 of us left.

General Miles

Nelson Miles rose from working in a store to being a general at the age of 26, during the Civil War. In the 1870s, he led armies defeating many tribes farther east than the Apaches, such as the Comanches. Miles used officers who knew Apache ways to negotiate surrender with Geronimo.

I am a wanted man on both sides of the U.S.-Mexican border. Geronimo is worth many dollars, dead or alive!

I will sit down
and talk to
General Crook,
but the only
one I will
surrender to is
General Miles.
He is the one
I trust.

Surrender

Today, in the year 1886, we surrendered. I hated surrendering, because we had been the last free Apache. We came to the camp of General Miles in Skeleton Canyon, Arizona. Miles talked to me man to man, as equals. We took an oath not to do any wrong to each other or to scheme against each other. I believe him when he says the Apaches will be protected by the U.S. government and we will be given houses, horses, and land.

Miles:	"My brother, you have in your mind how you are going to kill me, and other thoughts of war; I want you to put that out of your mind, and change your thoughts to peace."
Geronimo:	"I will quit the war path and live at peace hereafter."

Prisoners

We knew we would be prisoners, but we expected better treatment than this. Around 450 of us were loaded into train cars without windows. Inside it was hot, crowded, and stank, since our only toilets were buckets. We traveled for days like this. Now I am in Fort Pickens in Florida, forced to cut logs every day. Most of the other Apaches, including my family, are in a different fort. I miss them terribly. Today, they gave us fish again. Why do they not know that eating this is taboo for Apaches?

We had few chances to breathe fresh air outside the train cars on that dreadful train journey from Arizona to Florida.

Prisoners of war

When Geronimo surrendered, General Miles agreed that the Apaches would be allowed to return to their home in Arizona after two years as prisoners. But the U.S. government held them as prisoners of war for 27 years, and their lands were taken. The Apaches were not charged with any crimes and had no chance to plead their innocence in courts of law.

In Alabama

It is now 1888, and I feel I have failed my people. We should be in Arizona now. Instead, we were sent to the Mount Vernon military reservation in Alabama. I have the joy of being with my family again. But it is even worse to live here. It rains all the time and freezes in winter. A quarter of the Apaches have died from illnesses such as tuberculosis and malaria.

> "The mosquitoes almost ate us alive. Babies died from their bites…[O]ur people got the shaking sickness…We had our own Medicine Men, but none of them had the Power over this malaria."
>
> Eugene Chihuahua, Chiricahua Apache prisoner of war

Fort Sill

Hundreds of Chiricahuas had to die before we were moved to the Fort Sill military reservation in Oklahoma in 1894. Captain Scott, who is in charge of the fort, has given us houses, clothes, and fields of our own. I have even started to go to the white men's Christian church. But there are many things I do not like here, such as when my children are hit by teachers at school if they speak the Apache language.

"There is no climate or soil which, to my mind, is equal to that of Arizona. We could have plenty of good cultivating land, plenty of grass, plenty of timber, and plenty of minerals in that land which the Almighty created for the Apache."

Geronimo

This reservation is a better place to live for the Apaches, but it is still not my true home.

Becoming a celebrity

It is strange to me that in my old age I have become so famous among the white men. Crowds cheer and applaud me when I appear in Apache clothing and rope horses or shoot bows and arrows in front of them at Wild West shows. At events like the St. Louis World's Fair last year, they line up to meet me, pay for photos of me, and even pay for buttons off my shirt! It is good to know my name will live on even after my death.

Displaying Geronimo

The U.S. government displayed Geronimo when he was a prisoner to show their superiority over the Apaches and other American Indian people. He was escorted to events by soldiers. Geronimo earned more money than he had before and became famous.

Geronimo was part of the parade for the new U.S. president, Theodore Roosevelt, in 1905.

Geronimo's Legacy

Geronimo never got to see Arizona again. He died at Fort Sill on February 17, 1909, from pneumonia. He was 80 years old. He was buried in the Apache Cemetery at Fort Sill. The other Chiricahuas did not leave the fort until 1913. The U.S. Army started to use the reservation as an artillery training ground. The U.S. government gave the Chiricahua the choice of staying near Fort Sill, where there was opposition from local non-Apache, or moving to the Mescalero Apache reservation in New Mexico. Two-thirds chose New Mexico.

Grave robbers

In 2009, descendants of Geronimo demanded that his remains be returned to his birthplace, in the Gila Mountains. A proper Apache burial would set his spirit to rest. Geronimo's remains include what is buried at Fort Sill and also his skull, which the Apaches claim was dug up and removed by grave robbers during World War I.

Before his death, Geronimo had become a Christian farmer living in a brick home. Yet he longed to return to his Chiricahua homelands and Apache lifestyle.

The struggle continues

Apaches and other American Indians suffered poverty and hunger for decades as they were trapped on reservations that were often on poor land. In 1924, American Indians were finally recognized as U.S. citizens. Today, there are over 2.5 million American Indians in the United States, including 30,000 Apaches. Most Apaches live on 13 reservations, many located partly on original tribal lands, each with its own tribal government and laws. Many tribes still struggle for ownership of ancestral land and for equal opportunities.

Today's Apache mostly live on or near ancestral lands. They uphold and retain some traditions while living modern American lives.

"Let me die in my own country, an old man who has been punished enough and is free."

Geronimo

Timeline

1829   Goyathlay is born in June to Taklishim (father) and Juana (mother)

1844   Taklishim dies, and Goyathlay takes on the role of caring for his mother and siblings

1846   Goyathlay is 17 years old and joins the Bedonkohe Council of Warriors

1847   Goyathlay marries Alope of the Nedni band of Chiricahuas

1848   The United States defeats Mexico in the Mexican–American War and then claims the Spanish southwest, including parts of the Apache territory in New Mexico

1858   Massacre at Casas Grande, Mexico: Alope, Juana, and Goyathlay's children are killed, along with many other Chiricahuas; Goyathlay and Chiricahua forces defeat the Mexicans at Arispe; Goyathlay is known as Geronimo from around this date

1861– 1865   The Civil War is fought

1863   Mangas-Coloradas dies and Geronimo becomes leader of the Bedonkohe Apaches

1872   The U.S. government establishes the Chiricahua Apache reservation in southern Arizona

1874   Cochise, leader of the Chokonen, dies

1876	The U.S. government orders all Chiricahuas to move to the San Carlos reservation in Arizona
1877	Geronimo is captured and taken to San Carlos
1881	Geronimo escapes with a group of Apaches to live in the Sierra Madre Mountains bordering Mexico and the United States
1886	Geronimo surrenders on behalf of the Chiricahua Apache to General Miles at Skeleton Canyon, Arizona; Chiricahua become prisoners of the U.S. government. Some, including Geronimo, are sent to Fort Pickens, Florida, while others, including Geronimo's family, are sent to another fort.
1888	Chiricahuas are moved to Mount Vernon, Alabama
1894	Geronimo and remaining 295 Chiricahua are moved to Fort Sill, Oklahoma
1904	Geronimo appears as part of the St. Louis World's Fair
1905	Geronimo rides as part of U.S. President Theodore Roosevelt's inaugural parade
1909	Geronimo dies of pneumonia at Fort Sill
1913	Remaining Chiricahuas finally leave Fort Sill

Fact File

American Indians are people who are indigenous to—or originally from—the Americas. The name *Indian* began to be used because Christopher Columbus, the European who first "discovered" America in the 15th century, thought the land he had found was connected to the Indies in Asia!

After the Europeans

When the first European explorers and colonists arrived in North and South America around Columbus's time, there were approximately 90 million American Indians, of which about 10 million lived in the present-day United States. These initial populations soon shrunk for a variety of reasons: war; famine owing to changing land use; slavery and other forms of forced labor; and new diseases introduced by the colonists, including smallpox and measles.

Diverse cultures

There are many different cultures of American Indians in the Americas. They are divided up based on factors such as the area they live, their language, and their use of natural resources. For example, peoples of the plains collected and grew grain, but those near the Arctic hunted seals. There are nine cultures in North America, including the Apaches and the Iroquois.. Many American Indians live in reservations today, while others live in towns and cities throughout the United States.

Write Your Own Journal

Geronimo is an important historical figure of interest to many people. You are already important to your family and friends and, who knows, you might be famous in the future! Everyone's story is of interest, and that is the purpose of your journal. It is not just a photo album and not just a diary. It is a combination of images and text that will capture both the ordinary and the unusual moments of your life. One day it will help you remember clearly what you have been up to, who was involved, and how you have felt through the years. Here are some points to consider when starting your journal.

On paper

Some journals or scrapbooks are created on paper. First, decide how big you want your journal to be. You can buy bound notebooks or scrapbooks of different sizes. But you can also make your own from folded large sheets of paper with thicker cardboard on the outside. Bind the spine using ribbon or string pushed through holes made with a hole punch.

You could also use a three-hole folder with loose, punched sheets of paper put in. The advantage of this is that you can add more pages as you create the journal and also different types of pages. For example, there may be plain pages for sketches, envelopes containing tickets, programs, or other souvenirs, as well as lined pages for neat handwriting.

On screen

Other journals are created on a computer. There are several advantages of onscreen journals over paper ones. For example, you can type in and edit what you have written, scan in photos, load digital images onto pages, and easily shift images around and change their sizes. You can also make identical copies of what you have made to give to friends or family. However, you may not always be near a computer to keep this sort of journal up-to-date, and if there is a power outage or you forget to save, your precious memories could become unavailable, or even lost!

Glossary

ambush hide and wait for somebody or something, then surprise or attack them

band in American Indian tribes, a group of related families living in the same area and part of a larger tribe

Bedonkohe band of the Chiricahua tribe

blood brother person related by birth or a friend sworn to be treated as a close relative

Chiricahua tribe of the Apache people once located in Arizona, New Mexico, and northern Mexico, now living mostly in New Mexico and Oklahoma

Civil War war in the United States from 1861 to 1865 between the northern states (the Union) and the Confederate southern states

communal shared by many people who usually live together

context background to a situation that helps us to understand it

council group of people elected or chosen to give advice, make rules, and govern an area or community

extinct when a type of living thing has died out and is no longer in existence. For example, woolly mammoths are extinct.

forefathers ancestors; people from a person's family in the past

gored wounded by a sharp horn or tusk

malaria disease causing fever and shivering that is transmitted in some parts of the world when someone is bitten by mosquitoes

medicine men people believed to have healing powers, the ability to communicate with the dead, and the ability to predict the future among American Indian cultures

mescal type of spiky desert plant with fleshy leaves. It is used as food and to make alcoholic drinks by American Indian tribes in the southwestern United States and Mexico.

moccasin type of soft, flat shoe with large stitches at the front. Moccasins worn by American Indians in the past were made from sewn buffalo skin or deerskin.

Nedni band of Chiricahua Apaches that lived near the Bedonkohes

peace treaty agreement between two or more opposing sides to stop fighting or war

pollen powdery grains produced by flowers to be used in plant reproduction to make seeds

reservation area of land in the United States kept separate for American Indians to live in

scalp remove the hair and skin from the top of someone's head

symbolize object, shape, sign, or other representation that stands for something else. For example, for Apaches, eagle feathers symbolize bravery.

taboo when something is forbidden or discouraged by a group of people or culture because it is considered offensive or embarrassing

tepee type of tall, cone-shaped tent usually made from poles and animal skins or canvas

tribe group of people with the same ethnic background and culture, including customs, language, religion, and foods, in common

tuberculosis infectious disease, usually of the lungs, caused by a bacterial infection

war whoop cry or yell made by American Indians during or after an attack

Wild West show traveling performance from the 1880s onward, featuring horse riding, shooting, actors, and American Indians, that represented the colonization by white people of formerly American Indian lands

Find Out More

Books

Behnke, Alison. *The Apaches* (Native American Histories). Minneapolis: Lerner, 2007.

McIntosh, Kenneth. *Apache* (North American Indians Today). Philadelphia: Mason Crest, 2004.

Moody, Ralph. *Geronimo: Wolf of the Warpath* (Sterling Point Books). New York: Sterling, 2007.

Sonneborn, Liz. *The Apache* (Watts Library). New York: Franklin Watts, 2005.

Sullivan, George. *Geronimo: Apache Renegade* (Sterling Biographies). New York: Sterling, 2010.

Web sites

www.indians.org/welker/geronimo.htm
Learn more about Geronimo on this site.

www.let.rug.nl/usa/biographies/geronimo
You can read the full autobiography of Geronimo, as written down by S. M. Barrett, on this web site. Note that some of the dates and accounts Geronimo gives are not accurate, but they were told when he was in his late seventies, in 1906.

www.native-languages.org/apache-legends.htm
"Coyote gets rich off the white man" and "Why the bat hangs upside down" are just two of the Apache legends you can read on this web site.

southwestcrossroads.org/record.php?num=521
Discover more about traditional Apache life on this web site.

Places to visit

Fort Sill National Historic Landmark and Museum
435 Quanah Road
Fort Sill, Oklahoma
sill-www.army.mil/Museum
The Fort Sill National Historic Landmark and Museum
preserves the area where Geronimo spent his final days.
Different buildings and exhibits give a sense of what life was
like there. Geronimo's grave is also nearby.

National Museum of the American Indian on the National Mall
Fourth Street and Independence Avenue, S.W.
Washington, D.C. 20560
OR
National Museum of the American Indian in New York
Alexander Hamilton U.S. Custom House
One Bowling Green
New York, New York 10004
nmai.si.edu/home
Visit either location of the National Museum of the American
Indian to see amazing exhibits of American Indian artifacts
and history.

Index